Return to Pretty

CAITLIN WILSON

Return to Pretty

Giving New Life to Traditional Style

Photography by Katie Nixon

Abrams, New York

*Dedicated to my grandmother
"Mare": The world was more
beautiful with you in it. Your touch
always made everything "pretty."*

*And to my mother, Kathryn——
your support and encouragement is
the ultimate expression of love.*

The POWER of Pretty

❈

My original hand-calligraphed mission statement said it all. Hanging on the wall of my first tiny little retail shop on Sacramento Street in San Francisco, it read: "Home should tell a story…of who you are, where you've been, and where you are going."

You see, I believe that your home can and should be a sanctuary—a special, layered, and meaningful place that feels like you are where you belong. That's one of the reasons I spend my days designing beautiful textiles, rugs, and decor. All that we create at Caitlin Wilson carries this theme: Everything must be pretty. So for the last decade, I have built a company in constant pursuit of pretty. And even when it seemed impossible, it was worth it.

Pretty to me elevates even the simplest of spaces. It is feminine, classic, thoughtfully coordinated, and intentional. Pretty is lovely and soft. It always brings me back to my sweet grandmother, who kept skirted tables in nearly every corner of her home with silver frames atop, displaying family photos and portraits of her grandchildren. Pretty is more than a look—it's a feeling of familiarity, belonging, and unconditional love.

This triptych is of an old European library that feels magical and charming with pastel tones. With its sleek, modern frames, it combines the best of old and new.

That's why I've long believed that it is time for a beautiful awakening, to bring back elegant style and embrace traditionally beautiful interiors and details. As a young mother and entrepreneur, it might feel easier to throw out the concept of beauty and say "someday my home will be pretty" or "pretty just doesn't fit in this season of life," but the truth is, we need the intrinsic power of pretty details now more than ever.

People are returning to pretty because of what it does for our homes, our daily happiness, and our families. It's as inescapable as air because it's oh-so-powerful. In a world that can sometimes feel awash in shades of gray, impactful color palettes and pieces can give spaces a total metamorphosis. Part of it is that for a time we couldn't travel to visit ornate architecture in faraway locales, so we sought to bring their beauty home by embracing design choices with cultural meaning and storytelling. Even if you're not one for frills, you may find that a few layered, tasteful, pretty elements in your living spaces can put a pep in your step that was sorely needed. Classically designed elements—whether it's a Rococo mirror, a carved mantle, or a princely textile—really do a lot for a home, and a frame of mind.

Don't believe me? Try to think of the last time you had to attend an important event feeling less-than-polished. Perhaps you were internally frazzled about your to-do list or just couldn't get to the dry cleaners in time to pick up your perfect dress, so you had to settle for your second best. Chances are it impacted how you felt—and the same is true of your interiors. Like fashion, interior design gives us a chance to express both how we feel and how we long to feel. Even when you've dressed just one room to the nines, it's a transformative experience!

So I'm beyond thrilled that classic, traditional style is back and better than ever. Call it "grand-millenial" or classic prep, but we've come full circle and entered the world of the New Traditional. When the *Wall Street Journal* declared that "young people are being drawn to 'unmodern' things," I jumped for joy, as many of us have been waiting for our contemporaries to get back to what is traditionally beautiful. We're embracing femininity with florals on florals and adding trims and scallops wherever possible. (Proof I adore details: My own wedding dress was alternating layers of pleats and scallops! My old soul has always longed for a more sophisticated, refined style to return to the forefront of design.) Hand-painted floral chinoiserie is universal and creates the most elegant backdrop for formal spaces. Young designers and millennials are finding a refreshing beauty in the "old-fashioned," whether that means picking up a Louis XV bed at a local flea market or using their grandmother's sideboard in the dining room.

In this nook of our studio, you can see how our pillow patterns play off each other—balancing motifs and scale in diverse ways that always look elegant, thanks to their dressmaker details like bows and pleats.

"

Call it 'grandmillenial' or classic prep, but we've come full circle and entered the world of the New Traditional.

"

To me this return signifies a pivot toward maturity. It's the moment we let go of trends and embrace our own personality, accepting our individual styles and becoming comfortable with what feels beautiful to each of us on a deeper level. It's about how we want to feel and how the people we care about feel in our home. It's *personal*. Your home is meant to tell your unique story, and that story can't be told in an empty or meaningless space. Meaningful design incorporates your history and traditions. That's one reason why the grandmillenial revival went viral: we all desperately need that nod to our sweet grandmothers and the lost art of creating and seeing beauty all around us. Rooted in the warmth you felt at your grandmother's house, it's characteristically pretty and over-the-top feminine—truly cozy and one-of-a-kind. That's why I love standing behind the lovely and classic—and championing your most charming memories of "home."

In my first book, I hope you will discover ideas for how to pursue all things pretty. That includes decor advice (such as ways to incorporate pretty details into every area of your life, including pattern mixing, color palettes, place settings, and timeless pieces that evoke a connection to the past and are always worth the investment). But it also includes happiness-boosting lifestyle tips, like the importance of handwritten notes and personalized gifts that will undoubtedly bring joy to those you love.

Despite what we might think at first glance, pretty is about way more than looks. I believe that pretty is classic, feminine, chic, sophisticated, and lovely. It is a feeling of happiness, connection, and welcoming familial warmth. It shows thought, care, and attention to detail, and it is a physical representation of love and kindness. Powerful, indeed.

An inspiration board is vital to pull your muses together into one place and visualize the flow and aesthetic of your room. We wallpapered this corkboard with grass cloth.

Antique maps give any room a sense of provenance. *Opposite:* We gave this antique piece
a fresh coat of paint and new hardware for Collected by Caitlin. I fell in love with the petite
nineteenth-century prints above it for their hand-drawn French mat borders.

A floral upholstered chair can't get any more "grandmillenial," adding a soft blue cording for a fresh twist. Coordinating your pillows with your draperies or furniture is the ultimate statement. *Following pages*: I'm dressed in a Luciana Emilia gown that uses my very own Bluebelle Stripe silk. Fashion comes home in a stunning formal living room dressed in Caitlin Wilson style.

A classic shelfie! We are forever inspired by design books and historical influences,
such as this porcelain tissue holder. *Opposite*: Be sure to bring texture
and pattern into your kitchen as Kelley Lynn Design did here, whether in the form
of pleated shades or a Caitlin Wilson chinoiserie pillow.

CHAPTER

1

Pretty

SPACES

L ike the moment you inhale your first armful of freshly cut peonies each summer, stepping into a pretty room can be a transcendent experience. Décor might seem frilly and frivolous, but it plays a powerful role in our happiness. I find that even just *looking* at the interiors of history's great design maestros can elevate my mood. Take the brilliant Dorothy Draper, who gave West Virginia's Greenbrier resort (formerly a Civil War hospital) a happiness injection with lush banana leaf wallpaper, checkerboard floors, and plenty of pink. Or Albert Hadley, who gave Brooke Astor's personal library a glow up with gleaming red lacquered walls, brass trim, and a profusion of chintz. But longtime professional decorators and DIYers alike may find themselves wondering: What's the recipe for a pretty room that will stand the test of time, like the work of Draper and Hadley?

For me, the classical principles of symmetry and balance are a major key to lasting beauty. Part of their appeal is subconscious. Because they're found in nature, they tend to create a tranquil feeling. It doesn't take much, but having a symmetrical element eases your eye. For example, flank a gilt bathroom mirror with two ginger jars, or employ matching table lamps on either side of the sofa. I find that balance tends to come into a space at the very end of my design process, thanks to textiles and window treatments (when possible, hang draperies symmetrically on either side of the window). Like rugs, these elements can be very grounding.

Another must have for a pretty room? A focal point. Without one, it's too easy for a space to feel untethered. Living rooms often have a "star" built right into the architecture with the fireplace. But creating visual interest yourself is doable, too, with a riveting piece of art or light fixture. Stumped on what to look for? I often seek out pieces with circles within them; there's something about circles that's universally appealing, especially because they juxtapose perfectly in our square and rectangular rooms. (Look to my own small former foyer, on page 30, for an example—I hung a gilt iron ring chandelier above an Art Deco–inspired round table. Not only was it a warm welcome every time we came home, but it gave the room a purpose—and a place to set the keys!) Mirrors are another of my go-to's for creating a focal point. They are eye candy (especially when gilt and somewhat sculptural in shape), and they bounce even more light into a room. My friend Courtney Petit hung a sunburst over a mirror to make a double whammy focal point, and it blew my mind!

I love how my friend Courtney designed this foyer in her Dallas home. There is something whimsical about painting your ceiling the color of the sky; it lends a really nice balance to the space and gives you that "aha" moment. And her collection of Wedgwood china is nothing less than amazing!

66

For me, the classical principles of symmetry and balance are a major key to lasting beauty.

99

When it comes to picking finishes and putting pieces together, I've developed a freeing approach: *Rules were meant to be broken.* I learned that maxim for myself when I was just opening my flagship store in Dallas and chatting with Nick Brock, the antiques guru who has a shop next to ours. I asked him: "What are the rules for antiques? Am I allowed to pair a Gustavian dresser with a Regency mirror?" Back then, I was so concerned about doing everything right and following the time-honored design rules. He chuckled and said: "If you see them together and you like it, they're meant to be." In other words: Go for it!

Scale is another story. In designing your floor plan, try to err on the side of caution and opt for smaller pieces that fulfill your actual day-to-day needs. An oversized chair is almost always clunky and wrong in a space (not to mention a pain to move when it doesn't feel quite right). Unless you're seeking a deep, plush sofa to sink into for movie nights in your TV room, I love a swivel glider. Blame my grandmother, who always had a pair of them in her home. The French may have invented the *tête-à-tête* sofa in the early nineteenth century, but grandma knew best: Swivel gliders are so comfortable they encourage guests to linger and allow conversation to flow unfettered. It's the ultimate face time!

As I've matured as a designer, I find myself pulling back on too many contrasting elements in a room to up the ante on pretty. Years ago, I'd use contrast to be bold and "make a statement." But now I know that contrast can be as simple as using a different sheen or texture—and that such a subtle difference can be just as effective. It's a way to elevate spaces without being obvious. What's even more important is carrying a tone from room to room with complementing accent pieces, textiles, or accessories. You might, for example, install hand-painted de Gournay panels in your dining room and keep the adjacent foyer comparatively subtle, with complementary hues. The only thing better than a pretty room? Lots of pretty rooms!

For a special shoot at the Kips Bay Decorator Show House in Dallas, the addition of our Pasha rug and velvet pillows introduced a soft, lovely note to this room designed by Michael Aiduss.

It's always nice to have a surprise element. Here in my former Dallas foyer, we painted the door interiors a custom soft blue hue that played off the rug. *Opposite*: Antique-inspired cane back chairs bring a cozy texture to our former dining room. In fact, the whole room has a warm and enveloping textural feeling, thanks to the grasscloth walls, plush rug, and plaid wool drapery.

For a project in Salt Lake City, we paired an English roll arm chaise longue with
our Caitlin Wilson Anatole rug—the perfect reading perch. *Opposite*: In my store,
I hung our grass cloth floral wallcovering, Florentine. It was inspired by a
moment I had at the Gucci Garden in Italy, where I realized they combined refined
fashion with something a little bit edgy...and thus the stripes were born.
Following pages: Architectural symmetry makes a room feel extra grand,
especially when echoed in the decor. It solidifies the design.

Caitlin Wilson Blossom French Welt Silk pillows add a sheen and texture to this exquisite Courtney Petit living room, making the space feel very refined and layered.

There is power in a soft lilac, as seen in my own Dallas sitting room before we remodeled. The right combination of elements can create the loveliest home.

Above: The sophistication of checkerboard marble adds
an elegant grounding to Caitlin's own mudroom.
Opposite: Pretty meets practical in a space outfitted with
organization and functional details.

Patterns play off of each other in my own family room—a classic Caitlin Wilson color scheme of blues and blushes. I love a good check for a pop of contrast, and a subtle rug like our Desi in Blue.

A refurbished dresser gets a fancy coat of paint and gold striping, made even more lovely with a beautiful, balanced showcase of vintage plates above it.

Kelley Lynn Design of Dallas designed this exquisite living space, with its
chinoiserie pieces galore and arched windows that bring in abundant light. I especially
love the Caitlin Wilson Miriam rug and pillows, of course.

One of our most-loved patterns, English Garden, evokes a certain wild and romantic mood.

I love traipsing into the garden to cut fresh branches in the spring. Soft pinks bring such natural beauty into this space designed by Studio Thomas James. *Opposite*: There's always an opportunity for art, such as this diminutive seascape painting I found in a French antique store. Our Emma rug and Lucille lamp are a match made in French blue heaven.

A PLACE TO CALL HOME FARMER

THE ICONIC INTERIOR

Green is an underrated color. It always has a powerful impact and you don't need much of it but it goes a long way. *Opposite*: Courtney Petit's breakfast nook, with Caitlin Wilson Greek Key pillows. *Following pages*: This beautiful Dallas sunroom features our Grand-mère collection, which is a nod to my grandma, Marilyn ("Mare"), who really did make her own ruffled pillows.

Opposite: I couldn't help but go big when it came to ordering a range for
my cookspace, opting for a BlueStar range in pigeon blue.
Above: I brought Paris to my kitchen with my signature checked bistro stools,
which added an elevated European touch.

Don't forget to wallpaper your light switches, too, for an enveloping effect.
Opposite: This beautiful Dallas guest room has the cozy, layered feeling
of a European retreat, thanks to its antique bed frame with Caitlin Wilson
Marilyn pillows and our Lucille lamp on the bedside table.

2

Pretty

PATTERNS

M arie Antoinette's sumptuous bedchamber at Versailles is the aesthetic equivalent of cake (with a side of cake!). Gilt cherubs adorn the soaring ceiling; crystal chandeliers twinkle above; and—my obsession—a hand-woven floral pattern festoons everything from the walls to the stools to the bed's balustrades. Without that lavish motif to envelop the space, her bedroom wouldn't have been nearly as dreamy.

Marie must have known that more is *definitely* more. Even if you're not planning on practically tenting an entire space in one beloved pattern as she did, using beautifully designed motifs can add warmth to a home and bring a room to life. More than that, patterns are one of my favorite ways to tell a client's story. Like a picture, patterns speak a thousand words.

And yet, little strikes fear into the heart of DIYers and professional decorators alike as much as picking patterns. How do you select one you won't tire of within a week? And what's the trick to using multiple patterns in the same room, so the cast of characters doesn't compete? I've found what matters most is taking the plunge. If you're unsure of which design direction you want to take in your home, your hero pattern can be a tool that helps you choose the right path, whether you're going for preppy (cue the French ticking stripes!) or traditional (chinoiserie, at your service). Once your primary pattern is selected, it can kick off an entire interior—inspiring your color palette, furniture selections, and even the art. Just be sure to bring a swatch of it wherever you go as you're shopping; you'll want to have it on hand to see how well it jibes with other fabrics, finishes, and *objets*. I'll sometimes tote a pattern along with me for weeks, looking at it throughout the day in different light—even in the car—just to ensure I love it. As with any big decision, you need time to mull it over.

If you're anxious about mixing patterns of different scales and hues, know that you don't have to beeline to your nearest design center to thumb through 100 million fabric swatches. Just find that one hero pattern you can't live without and use it as a jumping off point for others around it. Rachel Ashwell's Shabby Chic brand ingrained in me my love for soft palettes and simple stripes. The fashion houses of Chanel and Hermès, to name a few, inspire me to be unabashedly myself and fearlessly feminine. A floral can be both fresh and nostalgic, exotic and traditional, colorful or neutral. Look for a clear, unmuddied color that's inspired by nature and it's more likely to go the distance. Most of what we design takes its color cues from gardens, florals, or the carefree pinks and blues of summer sunsets. Those natural colors are just easier to live with!

Paired with fanciful florals and woven in soft pastel hues,
age-old plaids can become unforgettable.
Previous pages: Our Vienna Floral pattern plays on a sophisticated European aesthetic
with its neutral palette and painterly, almost ethereal motif.

" Confidence is always in style. "

No wonder I've always subconsciously loved checks and plaids, in part because of my mother's Scottish heritage and in part because they evoke dewy trudges through the grounds of Balmoral. But I *consciously* love them because of their graphic, clean lines. They juxtapose so nicely against florals, it's like they were meant to be together. In a pillow arrangement of multiple textiles, it's vital to have some sort of "pop" within the array, like a pillow with trim, tassels, bows, or box pleat ruffles. It's like applying lipstick or a spritz of Hermès 24 Faubourg to finish your outfit—you're not fully dressed without it!

Some of my married clients have differences of opinion when it comes to pattern choice. That's to be expected. We understand when loved ones balk at eating certain foods, so why should we expect our significant others to be on board with a pattern just because we ourselves can't get enough of it? My advice: There's power in a pillow. You can always have a small cushion on an accent chair in your beloved fabric. It doesn't have to live there forever, but your partner should be willing to try it.

One other area where pattern is a must, especially if you have pets and children (but also if you find beauty as enchanting as I do): your rugs. I like to add as many colors as possible underfoot in my Persian rugs, because they're so much more versatile that way. The Caitlin Wilson–branded Kismet rug is our bestseller and has been since the day we launched it, in part because of that versatility.

Of course, if you're doubting your pattern decisions, do as Marie Antoinette did: Pick one motif and run with it, using the same fabric on the walls, draperies, pillows, and beyond. It might just be the most foolproof way to make a decorating impression, because it takes a certain level of confidence to pull off. And confidence is always in style.

Touch and feel our abundant rug options in our showroom.
Hand-knotted, low-pile rugs typically have more intricate detailing,
while our plusher styles offer a luxury feel.

A good rug can inspire the color palette of an entire room—especially one with myriad hues in it like our Jolie rug.

If you can't build your own Versailles, consider putting up a Francophile wallcovering, such as my Vivienne, with its flowers and ribbons. Surely, Marie Antoinette would approve!

A blue-and-white color palette is a forever classic.

"

Just find that one hero pattern you can't live without and use it as a jumping off point for others around it. Look for a clear, unmuddied color that's inspired by nature and it's more likely to go the distance.

"

Our hand-knotted Caitlin Wilson Kismet rug is a bestseller, thanks in no small part to its profusion of saturated tones. *Following pages:* A rug with many colors is a secret tool of designers, who often draw a room's surefire color palette from it.

The Penelope pattern is so vibrant and happy, it's like a barefoot garden picnic in June. *Opposite:* The only thing that makes a canopy bed even more precious in a little girl's room? Scallops.

There's something about combining woven rattans with buttoned-up patterns
that feels as natural and easy as a straw hat and caftan in St. Barts.
Opposite: Symmetry is powerful and helps cast a spotlight on beauty . . . such
as the sculptural tree trunks outside my former breakfast room.

Above left: A medley of pillows is almost always the right choice. In this little girl's
playroom, more is always more—especially when floral options are balanced by ticking tape.
Above right: A Caitlin Wilson collection will always have coordinating prints
and palettes—making it effortless for a client to mix and match.
Opposite: Our lead Caitlin Wilson artist, Nicole Ray, hand-paints many of our patterns
making each design truly unique.

There's truly nothing as charming as dainty wallpaper in a powder room; it turns even the smallest spaces into transportive experiences.

ENTERTAINING BEAUTIFULLY AERIN LAUDER

James Michael Howard ATMOSPHERE

CLASSICISM AT HOME

CHAPTER

3

Pretty

PILLOWS

My journey building the Caitlin Wilson brand has been a series of good luck and design miracles . . . and it all started with a pillow. Yes, a pillow!

Years ago, when my husband's career as an executive took us to live abroad in London, I would put our newborn daughter, Olivia, in a carrier and venture onto the Tube for our daily adventures together. We would often find ourselves lured into the nearest Cath Kidston store, where I was immediately and endlessly inspired. Cath's love of florals and patterns—and the way the entire shop would wrap us in color and thoughtfully designed, coordinating prints—became a transportive remedy for my homesickness. We would wander the shops of King's Road and Marylebone High Street, areas known for their high-end home stores adorned with lush, fresh florals and filled to the brim with English charm. I was hooked. Our strolls there stirred in my heart a deep, endless love for the patterns and textiles of home. To me, so much beauty lies in the colors and accents that enliven a room and create a cohesive color story.

After our two months in London, my family took off for our next adventure: Dubai. We found a great high-rise flat to rent in the glittering skyline of the financial district, but—typical for the area—it felt stark and sterile inside. Eager to make our life comfortable and reasonably beautiful, I instantly started working on the design of our first official home as a family. I scoured every design boutique in the mall only to find modern, meaningless decor and textiles. It took several trips to IKEA for me to realize that I was the only one who could create the warm feeling of home I was so desperate to feel—for myself. So I rolled up my sleeves and used my own resourcefulness to find a local seamstress. She helped me create black and cream pillows with Greek key tape trim that I could add to our living room. I also shared the pillows on my blog. Soon enough, the locals were asking me to make pillows for their homes, too. Before long, Caitlin Wilson Design was born.

I love all things porcelain. Ginger jars are especially lovely
in blues and pinks.

> "
> Whether graced with
> hydrangea or pink magnolia,
> each floral motif has
> all the energy of a walk in
> a dew-dotted morning
> garden—and gives a space that
> very necessary element of
> *je ne sais quoi.*
> "

Over the years of creating my brand, as I've continued to add project after project to my portfolio, a common theme developed. The concept of pretty became the foundation of nearly all of my designs. So it's no wonder Caitlin Wilson pillow textiles are always the epitome of fresh and feminine, with happy colors and balanced patterns. I have always aspired to fill a void or need in the design world, and find that pillows can have a huge impact—instantly! Early on in my design career, distinguishable pillows and patterns became my signature look—and while they're my passion, they've evolved into so much more: rugs, furniture, curated antiques and art, linens, wall coverings . . . the list goes on.

And yes—I still swoon for a good pillow. Because florals often tie an entire room design together, it didn't take long for lovely floral pillows to become a trademark element in my projects, and ultimately my brand. Whether graced with hydrangea or pink magnolia, each floral motif has all the energy of a walk in a dew-dotted morning garden—and gives a space that very necessary element of *je ne sais quoi.*

A well-appointed corner with a lovely spot
for floral pillows creates balance and adds soft color.

87

Combine various pillow patterns—those with structured motifs and soft florals—for the strongest effect. *Opposite*: Vivienne is one of my favorite patterns of all time; we designed it using an antique print I found. It's perfect paired with bold, graphic stripes.

The Sweet Regency collection inspired by small scale prints and elegant English florals.
Following pages, from left: A Swedish Gustavian daybed is even more charming with a
French mattress cushion. For us, a collection isn't complete without matches and playmates.
Shown here: the Vienna Floral, which goes perfectly with blush pink leopard print.

PILLOW GUIDE

Not all throw pillows are created equal. But because there are as many options as there are varieties of tulips, I've put together a few tips to know and love.

Embrace Odd Numbers

On a sofa, I recommend placing an odd number of pillows. If it's an oversized piece and you can fit five pillows, go for it, but even three works wonders.

Make It Measured

Depending on the height of your sofa, I like a 24 × 24-inch or 20 × 20-inch pillow on each side, and a lumbar pillow—16 × 26-inch, 14 × 20-inch, or 12 × 20-inch—in the middle. For chairs, 14 × 20-inch pillows are typically best.

Bed Down

Comfort is clearly queen in the bedroom. You'll want squishable, oversized back pillows for reading a book; two decorative pillows (I prefer the 24 × 24-inch size), and of course, monogrammed euro or king shams.

Stuff Style

Our go-to inserts are 90 percent down and 10 percent feather—but if you're allergic, know that poly-blend inserts have come a long way! Still, whenever possible, down and feather pillows are preferable because you can sink into them. Just don't forget to fluff them by tossing them up in the air and giving them a good karate chop.

A parade of Caitlin Wilson pillows.

I find blue and white florals look their best when they're placed alongside ginghams
and plaids in the same colorways; they make each other stronger.
Opposite: The hand-painted Highland Floral pattern can be used so many different
ways, from the wallpaper to the pillows.

Just one monogrammed pillow can make the entire
room around it feel more custom and tailored.
Right: A few of my favorites.

ENTERTAINING BEAUTIFULLY AERIN LAUDER

James Michael Howard ATMOSPHERE

CLASSICISM AT HOME

CHAPTER

4

Pretty

DETAILS

I magine if butterfly wings were simple, flitting around the air in one lone color, without any intricate motifs to adorn them. They wouldn't have quite the same allure, right? Or if the historic châteaux of France didn't look like fairytales, but were built entirely of concrete, steel, and glass. Would anyone travel across the globe to visit them? Of course the answer is no. When they say "the beauty is in the details," they're right!

It's a lesson I learned early on. When I was at university, I worked in a floral shop in a small Victorian home. It was painted white and blue, stocked with antiques, and reminded my then-boyfriend, Brigham, of a grandma's house. He meant it as a joke, but that Grandma Factor is exactly what I loved about it. There was a certain charm and appeal to me in the old, vintage-inspired décor. It felt like it had so much more meaning than the shapeless, commonplace pieces that were sold at other home décor stores. I felt a passion spark and began spending my paychecks month to month on furniture and *objets* for my home, which felt so much more long-lasting and worthy of a splurge than clothes.

When I moved into a new apartment each year, I was obsessed with decorating it. I would spend the first few weeks and months of the semester decorating and redecorating until each finishing touch felt perfect. By the time I landed in Paris at nineteen years old for study abroad, my fate was sealed: I knew I wanted to be a designer. The experience of traveling on weekends to château after château, from the Loire valley to southern France, had cast its spell on me. It was a whole new world of color, beauty, and lavish, layered details—in the tapestries, upholsteries, gilding, and art—and I was head-over-Louboutins in love. It was all so pretty!

In my years of learning about design and steeping myself in its centuries-old lessons, I've found that it's the teeny tiny details that really make a space. You can do so much with trims, textiles, and embellishments. Drapery and upholstery can be taken to the next level with the addition of a bullion fringe or a simple tape used in a fresh way. I love to create a chic look with grosgrain-type trim. It's simple yet striking, and you can use your imagination to create your own design and look. That's really how my business came about—getting creative with something that has been seen and done before, but doing it in a new way. My love for trimmings and tailored details came from my exposure to sewing and quilting at a young age. I spent my childhood through teenage summers in California, spending days upon days learning how to sew from my "Marmie," my best friend Elizabeth's mom. She was a perfectionist and mother extraordinaire who taught me, Elizabeth, and our friends— who all felt like sisters, because we were so close—how to sew everything we could imagine. It's no wonder that her real name was Martha—she was a creative genius with sewing and cooking (I even have her chocolate chip cookie recipe memorized). We were like a millennial version of *Little Women*, sleeping three girls to a bed, staying up late into the night dancing, and sewing our hearts out! Those memories imprinted within me a love for details and the importance of a handmade touch. To me, the trimmings on a pillow add such an elevated, bespoke feeling, but they're not the only area where it's important to invest in the little things.

Placed on a sideboard, a bust like this one looks straight out of a Jane Austen period film's central casting.

"

Moldings are a powerful part of creating a traditional room. They draw the eye and are a necessary part of defining the architecture and era.

"

Another place I can't help but add detail is the walls themselves. Moldings are a powerful part of creating a traditional room. They draw the eye and are a necessary part of defining the architecture and era. Larger rooms can often handle substantial crown molding (the taller the ceilings, the more detail or trim is necessary to have the same impact). I prefer to use plaster molding in my own home, because it allows me to get the level of rich, intricate motifs that very few regional craftsmen know how to create today. It's incredibly elaborate, and just glancing at it can transport you instantly from Texas to the ornate châteaux of France.

No classically-leaning traditionalist will forget to add monograms to her home, especially if she lives in the South. I've added them everywhere from my girls' bed pillows to the valance of my bed canopy! Monograms are eternally sophisticated, and you can find tasteful, unexpected ways to apply them. The trick is to go for a bespoke monogram rather than something quickly found online that's more fitting for a boy's school backpack. There's art in monograms. Use a matte (rather than shiny) thread and have them embroidered on Belgian linens for a truly elevated look.

The design of a room is never complete until it is graced with the finishing touches: accessories, pillows, flowers, and otherwise styled tables and shelves. No wonder most designers call it their favorite part. It feels like a reward for getting through the harder, more daunting issues of painstaking measurements, sourcing, and deliveries. You can really pull together a design scheme with those small things—they really do add up! As a young designer I raided used bookstores with fabric samples in hand to source tomes with color-coordinating spines. Now that I have a more refined palette, I'm more intentional: I customize books and create products in truly unique colors for a result that is nothing less than spellbinding.

A large tray, such as this scalloped one we offer at Caitlin Wilson, can transform nearly any ottoman into a coffee table. *Following pages*: Antique furniture pieces juxtapose stunningly with upholstered modern ones, such as these X-benches paired with a centuries-old wedding cabinet from France.

105

Above: Small art pieces do wonders for a small space paired with seating or atop a credenza. If I fall in love with a small art piece when traveling, I know I'll always find the perfect place for it—especially if it's in a timeless gold gilt frame, such as with the intaglio above and the landscapes at right.
Opposite: Saturated art pieces bring in color and depth, even if they're not original. Grass cloth wallcoverings lend an elevated feel.

Blush chinoiserie is the epitome of feminine chic style in this stunning room designed by Alexandra Kaehler Design. *Following pages*: Chinoiserie is timeless and creates the ultimate backdrop. Use it wall-to-wall or inside wood paneling for a high-end hack.

Traditional chinoiserie murals can make a chic statement when paired
with the right pieces; pillows with a sheen or embellishment add a luxe touch.

The POWER of CIRCLES

Humans are naturally drawn to the geometry and
balance of circles. After all, they're in the sun,
the moon, and even our own eyes. The fact that they're
inherently balanced makes them easy to work with.
Here are a few of my favorite places to employ circles for
joy in the round.

TABLES

For me, a round table is almost always better than a
square one. In a living space, round side tables and coffee
tables balance the frequently square-shaped and
angular rugs and furniture. In a dining room, a circular table
puts everyone on equal footing, because there is no "head."

MIRRORS

A round mirror is very soothing and creates
such a nice focal point in a space—especially when you
surround it with symmetry.

LIGHTING

Often found in churches and castles like Versailles,
ring chandeliers feel historic and make a room
feel larger. Bonus: They spread light around better than
a single source.

TOPIARIES

Closely clipped plants have been beloved since the
days of ancient Rome and provide instant classical beauty.
You can pick up a myrtle or boxwood version at your
local florist and bring the allure of a French garden home.

I intentionally brought the beauty of a living space to our former primary bathroom
by creating my own special dressing corner, complete with a Louis mirror.
Opposite: Make your work-from-home desks as over-the-top beautiful as possible
and you'll always be wrapped in inspiration.

Above: Caitlin's new line of paints includes the perfect hue of François blue—
her signature pop of color—which is used here as a bold backdrop.
Opposite: An oversized seascape painting from my parents' collection added
a salty ocean view to our former living room.

Our Caitlin Wilson Francie crib has a laurel and ribbon motif, a signature of our beds that gives it a beautiful, classical detail. *Opposite*: The lilac stripes on this upholstered headboard provide a perfectly structured setting for the sea of florals in these Cait Kids sheeting.

Pretty
PROPER

I grew up within a family and extended family that truly valued manners and the centuries-old art of *politesse*. Case in point? When I was a child, my mother and grandmother taught me that a gift you've received isn't really yours until you've written the giver a thank you note. As with so many other things, they were right!

It is so important to be respectful in your interactions with others, and that's just as true in your interior décor sphere as well. That's one reason that I find the cinematic worlds of *Pride and Prejudice* and other Regency-period historical dramas eternally enthralling. I'll never forget watching my first Jane Austen movie in college and becoming enamored with the set design. It was so charming, with its petite florals and carved woods. Everything from the ornate textiles on the walls to the sumptuous silhouette of a scroll arm sofa told visitors and family members, at a glance, "I care."

Of course, as we all know, formality has practically flown out the window in much of our society. (Indeed, if she caught sight of our casual ways, Jane Austen herself would be aghast!) But there are ways to marry the comfort that today's ultra-hectic lives demand with a stately aesthetic. One of my favorites is to mix a few storied antique art or furniture pieces in with your modern things. Or to invest in beautifully detailed wallpaper, such as chinoiserie panels, that can add a rich feeling to any room. While Regency era ladies prized their oil portraits, I always have a table devoted to family photographs in polished silver frames incorporated into the design of my homes. There's nothing like a collection of old and new family photos set on one skirted table!

Another way to bring a sense of propriety into your home is to champion traditions in your daily life itself. My maternal grandmother was a huge influence on me and a wizard at holding onto the elements of previous eras that should be continued, even if you're not a card-carrying member of the British aristocracy. She was a very proper person, and she loved to set her table beautifully whenever guests came to call. To prepare before an event, she would arrange her tablescape the night or even several nights beforehand (turning the plates and glasses toward the tablecloth to evade dust), just so she knew everything was ready to go and perfectly arranged. It's a trick my own mom uses to this day. Dear friends of mine in Texas have inherited their grandmothers' tableware and used it to begin their own lovely collections, something I'm also doing myself so I can continue to properly set my own tables.

Previous pages: In this stunning Highland Park, Texas, home with very formal interiors, a striped settee provides that chic element that makes it fresh. *Opposite*: It doesn't have to be Easter brunch to be a special moment—even everyday entertaining should be memorable. For us, it's sparkling lemonade and candlesticks twinkling on the table.

"

Like my grandmother, I like to use handwritten notes as an opportunity to bring meaning into my life and touch the lives of others.

"

My grandmother adored using place cards to arrange guest seating, putting thought and care into each dinner party or afternoon luncheon to maximize sparkling conversation! Even at simple Sunday suppers, every guest at her table felt cared for and loved. One of her go-to moves was to make a personalized cookie bearing the name or nickname of each guest, written with frosting in her trademark penmanship. It was an over-the-top thrill, and always unforgettable!

Grandma also had a special talent for wrapping gifts. We would set up a wrapping station during her Christmas visits and spend hours (and hours!) together until each present looked worthy of both the occasion and the loved ones she so cherished. She wrapped presents in such beautiful ways—with exquisite ribbons and tags, and often with a final swaddle of cellophane. It was just so thoughtful! The wrapping made the gifts within all the more special. It's a tradition I continue to this day.

Like my grandmother, I like to use handwritten notes as an opportunity to bring meaning into my life and touch the lives of others. Each card you send is more than a thank you. It offers you a chance to say something meaningful and express your love for the receiver. Why bother sending a note if it's not going to make a difference in someone's day? Aim to write the kind of notes they'll savor, then pin up on their inspiration boards or tuck away in their scrapbooks to keep forever. Anything less is a waste of a stamp. A proper lifestyle or home isn't intended to be stuffy. It's more about thoughtfulness: showing up for friends and family with the TLC we all deserve. The sentiment behind a nice dinner set with place settings is showing care and love through attention to detail, and ultimately setting aside time from your busy schedule to be together and gather. And trust me: when you up the ante on "pretty" with each event you host, your guest's memories of it will be all the more magical.

We love monograms; they always add a special touch
and make people feel special.

Above: Take a moment every season to print out and frame a few of your favorite
recent family photos—little brings more joy to a tabletop.
Chinoiserie-inspired tableware compliments our Caitlin Wilson Canton Toile linens.
Opposite: This desk is a hand-painted Edwardian antique that we found at
Round Top and sold in our Collected by Caitlin series.

Draperies are a wonderful place to splurge with extra details—you'll feel luxurious every time you touch them. *Opposite*: The Asian-inspired twist in this clean-lined coffee table provides a surprise element that adds oomph and makes the otherwise frilly space more approachable.

A proper dining room in Jada Leigh Mowles's home featuring my Eliza hand-knotted rug.
Petit fours are very proper and were invented in nineteenth-century France.
Opposite: I love the timelessly alluring elements of the garden in this dining room, from
the bee napkin rings to the lattice chairs and chinoiserie walls.

Our Caitlin Wilson Dallas showroom is stocked with feminine touches, including brass-trimmed furniture and tassel-skirted sofas. The many muted tones of our Blush Aviary rug allows for flexibility in the overall design concept.

There's nothing like starting the day on a beautiful note. Create a "skyline" on your table using elements at various heights for a sumptuous feeling and visual interest. Fenwick Fields' lovely linens in Jada Leigh Mowles's sweet breakfast nook creates a sweet brunchscape with mix and match layering.

A built-in corner cabinet in Courtney Petit's Dallas home is a prime display
of our prettiest Caitlin Wilson glassware. *Opposite*: A stunning tabletop by Courtney
from her impressive dish collection layered with scalloped linens by Fenwick Fields.

THE WELCOMING HOUSE JANE SCHWAB AND CINDY SMITH

James Michael Howard ATMOSPHERE

Opposite: Pink is forever cheerful for a playful afternoon tea.
Above: Create a gorgeous moment for any corner or festive table by using several types of flowers in vases of different heights, shapes, and sizes—one of my tricks of the trade.

6

Pretty

PALETTES

Anyone who doubts the transformative power of color can find proof of its magical powers in Charleston, South Carolina's Rainbow Row. In 1931, the thirteen eighteenth-century homes looked down on their luck: tattered and dreary. Until, that is, homeowner and preservationist Dorothy Porcher Legge decided to paint her exteriors pastel pink. Neighbors followed suit with their own happy hues, and soon the entire street was adorned in colors that summon the macaron flavors at Ladurée: rose blossom, pistachio, *framboise*. Almost a century later, the once-humble promenade of buildings has become Charleston's version of the Eiffel Tower. People come from across the globe to see it (and, let's be honest, Instagram it). And all it took was paint!

Color impacts the way you feel in your space and in your surroundings. Whatever you're trying to portray, the right hues can be a powerful means of expression. I've known the importance of color since I was a child, decorating my bedroom with periwinkle walls here, seafoam accents there. Later, living abroad in Paris, London, and Dubai with my burgeoning family, I found so much comfort in color. When the executive high-rise flats we rented in Europe and the UAE felt cold, I knew I could bring in a sunny, warm feeling with the right textiles and accessories. Even on the drizzliest, most overcast days, having a colorful interior was life-changing. It meant that coming home was like stepping into exultant technicolor rather than staying mired in a slick, soulless world of corporate greige. A dream.

Now as a seasoned designer, I have my go-to colors that have evolved over the years: navy blues, lavenders, and pinks as joyful as a cherry tree in bloom. I almost always employ at least two colors in a palette to give a room richness and depth. Because I love my textiles, I often select a "hero" to build a room's palette around—usually a floral that kicks off a complementary color scheme, like pinks and purples. If you're nervous about choosing complementary hues, take a peek at the color wheel, which was invented by Renaissance-era physicist Sir Isaac Newton and is still an invaluable tool today. To find complementary tones that will work together, pick your chosen primary hue—say, a violet blue—and look at what's opposite of it on the wheel (in this case, a zingy Hermès-orange). Flawless! Another trick I'll use is to look at color pairings through the lens of a fashionable floral dress—if you consider hues from that angle, you'll see whether they play well together or not.

Previous pages: This is one of our most-loved images, and I can see why it gets so much attention. The color, Benjamin Moore's Nickel, is perfect—and totally revived the outdated cabinets. *Opposite*: Here I am in my studio, hard at work on my new paint collection. Remember, don't trust the colors you see on a computer screen! To truly get a feel for a hue, you have to hold it in your hands, which is why ordering fabric swatches and paint samples is always worth it.

> ❝
> # Whatever you're trying to portray, the right hues can be a powerful means of expression.
> ❞

People often struggle with where to even begin when it comes to selecting their palettes. If you're having a hard time settling on a starting color, go find a fabric that you totally love on a piece of clothing or a throw pillow and use that as your muse. For me, that's the first task because it inevitably launches the rest of the room and all the colors and patterns surrounding it. A piece of art or cherished antique *pièce de résistance* can inspire you, too. If it has special meaning for you, it will be all the more beautiful. Just pull hues from it to kindle your wall color, rug, and beyond. When my friends and customers struggle to select a color palette for their rooms, I often tell them to choose what they have in their closets. Living in the colors you look good in almost always works. But what if you fling open your wardrobe's doors to find a veritable rainbow of dresses inside? In that instance, I recommend imagining yourself professionally photographed on the cover of a book or magazine. What would you see yourself wearing—and what colors would surround you? Designing with your dreams in mind can help you create a signature palette and style that compliments both you and your life.

When you're designing a whole home, you may want to settle on a theme of some sort and carry it throughout, so one space flows to the next—such as carrying one color from your living room to the adjoining foyer for a seamless effect. Fabrics are a great way to achieve that. One of my favorites is silk—it adds so much depth and sumptuousness, and feels so good in a space. It doesn't have to be overly shiny or fancy; even matte silk has an elevated aesthetic. When it comes to fabrics, I love wools and velvets, too; they're equal parts luxe and cozy. Couldn't we all use more of that in our lives?

When I'm pulling together a room's color palette, I'll often toss in a surprise shade. It's a move that can make everything feel more layered and authentic—like it was created over time, not over-nighted to your door from a showroom. Ralph Lauren is a maestro at this; he will frequently add a burnt orange or teal. They couldn't be further from my most beloved colors, but there's something about that subtle accent that adds to an interior immensely. The best spaces have unexpected elements; that's the difference between standard-issue interiors and those that were put together by a skilled designer. It will feel collected, like it's taken a decade to create.

If you're nervous about using color or just want to dabble in it without taking much of a risk, go for blue. This flat lay shows how beautifully blue compliments other colors, such as pastel pink.

CAITLIN W WILSON

This room was very neutral before we brought the rug and pops of blue in, and the color totally elevated the space—creating a luxurious, high-end feel with just one additional hue.

CLASSICISM AT HOME

Lavenders and periwinkles combine in our lovely Pasha rug to create a serene bedroom.
There are a lot of patterns here, but because they're all in the same palette and
tones, they feel restful. *Opposite*: We work very hard to balance the colors in our rugs
so that they complement our other patterns and accessories.

I adore this space, designed by Morgan Hunt and styled with Caitlin Wilson products,
including our Simone rug in Caramel. Morgan went bold with the jewel-toned
turquoise trim; the caramel carpet underfoot grounds the room with a warm foundation.
Following pages: The rug helped drive a sweet and sophisticated palette in
my daughter's former bedroom. For a cheerful nursery that can transition easily to a big girl
room, consider paneling the walls and wallpaper above with a bit of floral heaven.

PRETTY in PINK

I've used pink so much over the years that it has become part of my brand. Blue is my classic color, but pink is its perfect complement. When I run into other designers at the market, I inevitably hear: "Oh, you're the pink and blue lady!" Here, some of my hard-won wisdom from the pink frontier:

• Adding a little bit of pink goes a long way. Keep a delicate balance; you don't need to go overboard.

• Pink paint is especially difficult to navigate. You have to be careful to not choose something too powdery or too "Pepto Bismol." If I'm using a pink hue on the walls, I tend to go for one with a bit of a champagne or purple tint to it. You don't want it to look "baby" pink, even in a nursery.

• Using pink is an easy way to be chic. If that's your personality (and I know it's not for everyone!), try it on your laundry cabinets, or in a parade of happy pink pillows. People will love it.

• Dip your toe into pink with a few accents, such as our pink velvet pillow, which we can't keep in stock, it's so chic! Even a book with a pink cover or a lipstick pink garden rose on your entry table will do the trick.

Blush pinks bring such joy to a space—seen in the playroom above and my daughter's former bedroom, right.

No one is too young to appreciate a bursting bouquet of freshly cut flowers on their bedside table. *Following pages:* We painted this Gustavian desk a lovely shade of gray blue rather than leaving it in its wood finish. The result is soft and sophisticated, and really feels nice atop a patterned rug. Flaxen hues and blues are a peaceful pairing.

ROOMS FOR LIVING SUZANNE RHEINSTEIN

SIMPLICITY NANCY BRAITHWAITE

CONTRERAS DREAM DESIGN LIVE

THE ART OF ELEGANCE MARSHALL WATSON

Windsor Smith HOMEFRONT

No room is complete without a cozy throw blanket and at least one
small flower arrangement. Hydrangeas are one of my florals of choice; properly
cut and watered, they seem to last forever.

Above: The only thing better than a botanical print? A citrus botanical print, complete with a free-flowing ribbon. *Opposite*: I love a jewel box of a library, especially one like this, with its gleaming paneling and built-ins all painted one rich hue. When the lights come on after nightfall, it practically glows.

166

Ginger jars have been beloved since 221 BC, when they were used for storing, yes, ginger. *Opposite*: This sunroom feels like an al fresco space, thanks to its woven wicker pieces and latticed walls. *Following pages*: Some of my favorite blues have a slight whisper of green in them.

CHAPTER

7

Pretty

PIECES

I f you're a jewelry fan, you know that sometimes one gorgeous piece is all that you need to transform your entire look. Even the most frayed, timeworn denim jeans and a standard T-shirt can look exquisite with the right pair of chandelier earrings! The same goes with interior spaces. Just one show-stopping furniture selection can give an architecturally lackluster room all the head-turning capabilities of Château de Montrésor.

As a budding designer, I was often drawn to white; I didn't necessarily go for a collected feel. But over time, I realized how vital it is to have varied finishes in a space. Coming back to the United States from our expat life abroad, I couldn't help but notice that all the modern manufactured furniture available had a banal sameness: smooth, clean lines and boxy silhouettes. There's a time and place for having simple things, but will anyone treasure these in one hundred years—if they even still exist at all? As I matured in my taste, I became drawn to classical furniture pieces in interesting silhouettes from around the globe.

After our years in Hong Kong, something wonderful for an antique obsessive happened: We transplanted ourselves to Philadelphia. Living in a city founded in 1682 gave me access to the types of treasure that seems especially abundant along the Eastern seaboard: Federal-era secretaries, Duncan Phyfe cabinets, and more. I'll never forget the Regency dining set I discovered on Craigslist. It was only one hundred fifty dollars, yet adding it to our first apartment back in the States felt like we were making ourselves a truly "grown up" home. To this day, I still love to begin with a clean palette and add in pieces in warmer wood tones in traditional silhouettes. It matures a space and gives it history, richness, and depth. Start with one, then complement it with upholstered pieces (prioritizing comfort is a must!).

Previous pages: I can't get enough of the detail on this wedding cabinet
I bought from an English antique hunter who'd unearthed it in France.
Opposite: At Nick Brock Antiques, our next-door neighbor shop in Dallas.

> "
> A room's interiors can
> fall flat without a
> historical case good or an
> item that has patina.
> "

Now that I've founded Collected by Caitlin, I often venture with my team to Paris, England, and secret spots around Europe to scour for these types of unforgettable pieces. Among our many finds, we've discovered carved Venetian-style armchairs with their original sunny yellow upholstery intact; a carved marble bust by nineteenth-century Florentine sculptor Guglielmo Pugi; and a nineteenth-century English Adams-style secretary that was intricately hand-painted with ribbons and flowers. The thrill of the hunt is half the fun, but the results are, in a word, *divine*!

If you're new to antiques, start by finding a reputable dealer in your area. It's smart to go and chat with them—not only to educate yourself, but also to develop your eye and make a connection. If you tell them you adore furniture from the Gustavian era, for example, they'll be that much more likely to reach out to you when a winning piece comes in their door, giving you first dibs. Looking for value? Proceed directly to consignment stores and estate sales, and go ahead and haggle—sellers expect it.

When I'm contemplating an antique piece, I consider where I'll be using it. Do the drawers have to open and function well, or will it just be sitting prettily at the end of a hallway? If you need the seamless functionality of modern drawers—which have markedly improved since the 1700s!—stick with something new. When you have young children and are weighing an expensive antique, be sure you'll be able to place it in a spot where it won't become a canvas for their Crayola scrawl. But above all else, don't be afraid! A room's interiors can fall flat without a historical case good or an item that has patina. I know I've said it before, but it really is like jewelry. When you invest in something timeless and special, you'll never regret it.

We painted the walls here in Benjamin Moore's Palladian Blue,
a timeless, historic-feeling color.

176

The beauty is always in the details, such as in this hand-carved
cabinet or brass table with a marble top, opposite.

Above: To achieve a twist on traditional furniture, paint the inside of an etagère with a soft, contrasting paint. Here, I used Nickel with White Dove by Benjamin Moore. *Opposite:* A painting from my personal collection provides a "view" over our refurbished antique nightstand.

The more deeply detailed the piece, the more I'm inclined to love it,
such as this Duncan Phyfe breakfront, above left.
Opposite: This demilune cabinet in Courtney Petit's home is a timeless beauty.

Before I remodeled it, my house had these great arched windows and a fresh green and blue color palette. *Opposite*: As long as you update the upholstery and cushions, most antique chairs can be just as comfortable as ones made today—and they're often more likely to last generations. A pop of painted green trim is a fun way to work with wallpaper—Jadite by Sherwin Williams, shown here, in Jada Leigh Mowles's study.

Antique desks provided enough storage for practically anything.
Opposite: A Swedish-inspired demilune table paired with rich wool drapery
and Caitlin Wilson Stonewash grasscloth.

Cornflower blues, pretty patterns, and pastels are Caitlin Wilson classics. *Following pages:*
A painted grass cloth chest is a Caitlin Wilson exclusive that's universally appealing,
thanks to its contemporary shape and warm texture. A Caitlin Wilson lamp atop a truly
unique piece—a flower-shaped antique table found by designer Morgan Hunt.

A Vienna Floral pillow
makes a centuries-old
chair modern. *Opposite*:
A vignette of fresh
accessories atop an
antique table.

8

Pretty

PLAYFUL

Muddy paws. Tiny, finger-painted hands. Golf cleats that refuse to give up the wet grass and wetter sand of the eighteenth hole. As much as we try to perfect our homes, life happens—and it should! Sometimes living life to the fullest means getting a little dirty. But that doesn't mean we can't prepare.

One argument for traditional interiors is that they hold up better than white-on-white modernist ones would. As a mother of five, I have seen it *all!* I've had pencil drawings on my chinoiserie wallpaper and pink medicine splashed all over the sofa when my little ones were ill. So I know firsthand that while minimal, milky rooms may look cool on Instagram or in a boutique hotel, they can be very hard to maintain in the real world.

For actual practical living, color, pattern, and traditional pieces are much more conducive to embracing the realities of daily life. Plus, performance fabrics have come such a long way in recent years that they are not only indistinguishable from standard ones, but they are practically spill-proof. Invest in a textured or directionally patterned performance fabric upholstery for your highest-traffic areas and you'll be able to relax a bit when the grape juice topples. If the fabric is too smooth or doesn't have any texture to it, you may want to rethink it—sometimes you need a bit of movement to trick the eye into glossing over mistakes (unfortunately, you can't undo a Sharpie—believe me, I've tried). I personally love to go for nubby upholstery, herringbone, and even mohair, which is fairly easy to clean. I'll also often layer with blankets and pretty throw pillows for extra protection. For your rugs, look for those with a lot of color—the more hues it has within its motif, the more kid- and drip-friendly it will be. Accidents happen, and you just can't cry over spilled milk forever, you know?

Each home my family has lived in told a unique, authentic story of the journey that brought us to where we are today. And no matter the size, location, or architecture, each one taught me to truly love the home I'm in while I was in it. Life's too short not to! The fact is, you can make any space "pretty" and all your own—whether you are living in a studio apartment in the city, settled in a sprawling suburban home, or presiding over a country pile worthy of a Jane Austen character.

Home is our sacred space, a place where our children play and rest. My passion lies in building a life where memories are happy and light. I want our home to foster creativity and learning, and most significantly, the boundless love that my children will carry with them forever.

Sailing, a nautical pattern we offer in a full bedding collection, is perfect for a nostalgic classic kid's space. *Previous pages*: In both wallpaper and bedding, Secret Garden by Caitlin Wilson provides such sweetness in a nursery.

> "
> Walls are the perfect place to create
> interest and drama in a children's space.
> "

When it comes to designing spaces for children, my personal style translates to refined palettes and sweet, nostalgic themes. It's a bit Old World—with a polished, tailored twist. My Caitlin Wilson Horse & Jockey Collection, for example, was inspired by the strong and beautiful horses I grew up with and later, vintage art from London's Portobello Road I bought when my son was one.

In playrooms and living spaces where your kiddos will have free rein, try adding as much storage as you can. I love using gathered fabric panels behind our glass shelving to hide the disorganized jumble of toys within. There are so many hacks that can help you tuck things out of sight in a pretty way. One of my friends recently skirted a U-shaped Ikea sofa that lifts up to reveal storage underneath, hiding toys and games without any clunky bins cluttering the playroom. She also skirted the train table so there would be a hidden stockpile of toys underneath. Genius!

Of course, setting the scene for a magical childhood is about more than practicality. Walls are the perfect place to create interest and drama in a kid's space. There is no better place to have wallpaper than the playroom because it saves you from having finger smudges and Crayola scrawls on the wall. Bigger, open rooms can be really hard to fill with art, and wallpaper can fill every nook and corner quaintly. A few of my favorite playroom patterns? Stripes, plaids, and cityscapes—each nearly as whimsical and enchanting as your little ones. Wallpaper is also the fastest way to create a theme and can set a transportive backdrop for your children's first memories. It adds interest to the walls without the worry of framed art pieces, which can topple—especially when play gets rowdy. Like your ceiling lighting, you can go a little crazy with it, because they're not going to be tugging it down.

When your kids are old enough to design their own rooms, I am in full favor of letting them—within reason. These are their sanctuaries where they dream their biggest dreams, after all. My mother was a great example of this, as she always gave me carte blanche to decorate my room . . . especially if it could be bought within the walls of a Laura Ashley store! But while some parents will let their child go all-in on a Star Wars theme, for example, I tend to steer my children just a bit toward choices that will last, at least for the major pieces and finishes. You want something that will grow along with them. Classic interiors are a better investment and less likely to be something they'll want to rip out when they go from their tween years to their pre-collegiate ones. If your child opts to add a themed pillow or lamp for a year or two, they can. It's what I call a win-win (and it won't require any dipping into their college funds).

In an older home with exposed beams overhead, our Bows and Blossoms
wallpaper feels very fanciful and fun.

Our Caitlin Wilson Leopold pattern is beloved for adding spirit and personality to a kid's room.

This Morgan Hunt–designed bedroom shows how green can be so powerful and playful.
Opposite: Our wallpaper Anniversaire is a very celebratory pattern. It combines
all the colors I began my collection with, ranging from orchid purple to punchy coral, and
of course plenty of blue.

Caitlin Wilson's Royal Crest pattern is very crisp and bold yet refined. Because
the rug, Archer, is tufted, it's a great option for a kids' space.
Opposite: Even a crib can benefit from a bedskirt, especially if it's scalloped.

Keep your child's personality in mind when designing their spaces.
Are they happy-go-lucky? Extra hard on their surfaces and finishes? Being practical is key.
Then, you can zero in on the appropriate upholstery and fabrics.
Shown here: Caitlin Wilson's Penelope pattern.

A miniature gallery wall of antique horse giclées is timelessly handsome.
Opposite: Our Horse & Jockey pattern gallops happily across the walls
of this charming little boy's room.

Designing for our daughters can be a challenge, whether combining bedrooms
or tying in coordinating prints and a color story. Make it playful and flexible,
but grounded in classic pieces and palettes. Our Caitlin Wilson pajamas are the
ultimate luxury for little ones and moms alike!

Previous pages: In the ultimate playroom hack, my friend Jada Leigh Mowles glamorized
IKEA pieces by adding skirts and Caitlin Wilson pillows. *Above*: Jada's knack for clever organization—
a kids cabinet's conceals color-coordinated books. The best part of the DIY project
on the previous page? Each storage ottoman-turned-sofa lifts up to reveal secret storage.
Opposite: Our Anniversaire wallpaper and Ada lamp makes a grandmillenial moment for a small space.

Opposite: Ava Rose is one of our bestsellers, and dreamy in a girl's room.
Above: Cleverly concealed by upholstery, this
cabinetry is very appealing to the eye and absorbs sound.

CHAPTER

9

Pretty

INSPIRED

In our Pinterest and Instagram world, inspiration can come from any source. But for me, there's nothing like the real thing. What can I say? I pride myself on being original. While scrolling the internet for ideas has its perks, there's nothing like jetting off to Europe to wander centuries-old castles and cobblestone streets if you have the means and opportunity. As a muse, it's simply unforgettable.

For my eighteenth birthday, my father treated me to an incredibly special trip to the Ritz London. I loved being ensconced in the hotel's neoclassical Louis XVI style grandeur—and the fact that former guest Jacqueline Onassis deemed it "paradise." Plus, it edges Mayfair, the West London district tucked alongside Hyde Park—a neighborhood that instantly felt like a second home to me, even though I'm not from there. When my husband and I moved to London briefly just after our daughter was born, there was nothing like exploring like a local. It just felt like the place I was meant to be! I'd carry our newborn in her BabyBjörn and set off for the 1852 Victoria and Albert Museum, or Designers Guild's exquisite, color-filled shops and find myself surreptitiously taking a day of inspiration, noting the British penchant for layered, historic interiors and floral prints.

Now, as a steward of my design business, a tastemaker, and a fervent believer in finding lessons from the past, I take my staff on frequent inspiration-gathering trips, passports in hand. I've always learned so much abroad, whether I was embracing my femininity by painting my room pink after my first stint in France, or seeking out my own pieces of chinoiserie—the seventeenth-century European interpretations of Asian originals—after seeing it so deftly employed within the tea room at the Mandarin Oriental Hotel in Hong Kong. Whether we're digging for buried treasure in France's Loire Valley or the Scottish highlands, these types of journeys result in the most meaningful takeaways. And they really resonate with clients.

Previous pages: An Italian bust I found for Collected by Caitlin, my curated line of antiques.
Opposite: Time for tea at Peggy Porschen in London's Belgravia neighborhood.

> # "
> # If you have yet to figure out what your own interior décor style is, my advice is to take your time and listen to your (design) heart.
> # "

I once had an interior design client who was a bit unsure of what her true style was. She often asked: "What do you think? What would be nice here?" We took her existing home as our inspiration to suss out her choices. But years later, fresh from a trip to France, she called us again—as a newly minted Francophile. She said, "I just came back from Paris and I was so inspired that I want to change *everything*. . . . I just want my house to feel like I live in France!" We did just that. While she may technically live in Texas, when you're within the walls of her home, you feel like you're at a seventeenth-century estate in Provence. You can practically smell the fields of lavender!

If you have yet to figure out what your own interior décor style is, my advice is to take your time and listen to your (design) heart. You can't base all of your decorating decisions off something you see online, or even on the bones of your home's architecture. You need to find the things that really, truly call to you. I've found that the most transformative way to do that is through travel. Whether it's a color, textile pattern, art piece, or specific design epoch, you may fall instantly in love and want to bring it home to use as a jumping off point for your own rooms.

When hops across the pond aren't in the budget (whether for financial reasons or because you just can't make it work within your calendar), turn to books. I've long been obsessive about design monographs because they're a much more intimate and inspiring way to immerse yourself in a designer's work than looking at Instagram. I could curl up with one for hours, like a novel! That's one of the reasons I've always cared so much about doing my own design book. And why I'm so honored that it's now in your hands.

A few of my favorite things create a beautiful mess, including doorknobs from my century-old house and inspiring colors.

VARVEL   **PROVENCE**STYLE   VENDOME
DECORATING WITH FRENCH COUNTRY FLAIR

Layers of artistry, including painting studies, at Caitlin Wilson's design HQ.
The Tuileries in Paris, designed in 1564.
Above left and opposite: Pieces from our collection with Provence Poiriers.

Details from our buying trip at the Marché aux Puces de Saint-Ouen and the
Ritz Paris, my favorite place to stay when I'm in town. *Opposite*: A sweet scene by
Alexandra Kaehler Design embodies the spirit of pretty.

Eye candy at the Ritz Paris and Musée Nissim de Camondo, a museum
dedicated to the French decorative arts. *Opposite*: Beautiful collected pieces
inside a hutch at Nick Brock Antiques.

229

The blue doors of London's Notting Hill always stop me in my tracks. Cabinets at
The Lanesborough hotel in Knightsbridge, London, which is set along Hyde Park. Tea time at the
Lanesborough is an iconic afternoon activity in one of my favorite cities. *Opposite*: Tiered trays
make anything you're serving more elegant because they provide the feeling of abundance.

TEXTILES
Where to Start

It's never been easier to purchase textiles, bed linens, draperies, and upholstered pieces, thanks to the seemingly bottomless options available on the World Wide Web. But if you aren't able to feel the cloth with your own hands before buying, it's well worth seeking out an Internet purveyor you trust. Even a cotton can go very wrong if it's not sourced and woven correctly! We curate every Caitlin Wilson textile option incredibly carefully. These are a few of my favorite textiles for touchable beauty.

LINEN
Over the course of my career, I've noticed that people are drawn to linen, a light yet sturdy fabric made from the flax plant. It's the most natural and can be very casual and livable. Go for a cotton/linen blend for fewer wrinkles.

COTTON
I love the formality of combed cotton! It's well worth an extra splurge because it's so much softer than untreated fibers.

SILK
Reportedly developed by Empress Hsi Ling Shi in ancient China, silk is supple, fanciful, and as regal as it gets. We have our silk patterns woven, which feels even better than printed silk—and is fabulous on window treatments and in your "pillowscape," especially if you have a little fun with stripes and bows.

VELVET
When "plush" and "cozy" are your goal, you can't do much better than this tactile short-pile option. Chenille has a ridged effect (fun fact: it's French for caterpillar!) and is incredibly snuggly on a sofa.

Details from Place Vendôme in Paris and the Ritz Paris, including intricately carved headboards and trim. (Is it any wonder Coco Chanel lived there for thirty-four years?). *Opposite*: You don't need to cut back on your ginger jar collection—especially when they look so fetching when displayed together.

Decor thrills high and low abound in Musée Nissim de Camondo.
Opposite: Bring home a Parisian note with ornate wall and crown moldings, which
can add so much luxury to a room.

RETURN
to
Pretty

"Pretty" hasn't always been the most popular design category, nor is it the look nor subject of the highest-trending videos on social media. Yet while minimalism and modern farmhouses have gotten much of the front-page action, there are a few of us who have steadily continued to design classically beautiful, pattern- and color-filled rooms for the ages. Call it what you may, but traditional taste is forever . . . and we are here for it! Unlike other interior design approaches that come and go, pretty is here to stay.

One reason it will never go out of style is that it's nothing less than a lifestyle. Many aesthetes have an inherent need to be inspired by the beauty in nature, color, and history—the types of things pretty rooms provide. These elements can bring us happiness, reminding us of the connections we have to each other and to generations past. There is nothing quite as lovely as a perfectly aged Louis Philippe mirror, as sweet as a Regency print on an early Gustavian bench, or as charming as a little trim or tassel on the edge of a curtain.

I'll always have a special place in my heart for symmetrically placed boxwoods, which conjure the seventeenth-century Ballroom Grove at Versailles.

And believe me, pretty is worth the effort. I've met so many people over the years of owning my brand who say they aspire to having a pretty home, but talk themselves out of it. They tell me their lives are busy and, inevitably, messy. But the fact is, every day is a gift. We shouldn't wait to have our beautiful home—or pretty guest room, or dreamy nursery. I promise you, it is within reach. My mission is to inspire people to do it now rather than to wait another day to live in a home that makes you feel truly happy. That's one reason I am so honored to be a part of homes everywhere. I get lovely notes all the time from people who have hung my wallpaper in their home office and discovered it made an enormous difference in their workday, or installed my bedding in their baby's nursery and found it brings them peace during all their late-night milk runs. Once you take that pretty plunge, you won't regret it!

When we design our homes, we're acting like a Hollywood set designer: creating the spaces where we will share some of our best memories with family and friends. As parents, creating a fortifying sense of beauty for our children to return to is key. It's just as Harold B. Lee put it: "The most important work that you will ever do will be the work you do within the walls of your own home." So, if you take nothing else from this book, take this: You have the power to make any part of your home—and with it, your life—pretty. You don't need to spend a fortune hiring a decorator to overhaul every corner of your house at once. Pretty can come into your day in little moments, from the just-cut lilac bloom on your bathroom vanity to the monogrammed pillows on your bed. The fact is, prettifying your interiors (and your world) is a collected process—and one that will bring you abundant, sacred joy with every single step. My life and career is evidence of the joy that comes from embracing your creativity. With each pattern, pillow, and product I design, it is such an honor to be in our most sacred spaces. It is a privilege to be alongside your pursuit for pretty—and to be a small part of homes all around the world.

Each of us has the power to create the lives we hope for and dream of, especially within our homes. May we each journey toward the powerful comfort, solace, inspiration, and connection we find in the gift of beauty that surrounds us—and return to pretty.

When in doubt, aim for symmetry. It is classical for good reason:
instantly serene and calming to the eye.

> "
> My hope is to
> inspire people to do it
> now rather than to
> wait another day to live in
> a home that makes
> you feel truly happy.
> "

Those real, pressed hydrangeas bring the eternal loveliness of the summer garden in. *Following Pages*: A collection of lovely things. So much inspiration comes from my travels in Europe.

244

What an incredible experience it has been writing my first design book, and it has truly been an honor to be a part of your homes. In the products and spaces I create, I take joy in every part of the process and I am humbled and grateful every day to do what I love. Writing and designing a book has always been a lifelong goal, and bringing it to fruition has been thrilling. My heart is full of gratitude for the many people I lean on every day in my life. I have an incredible village of support.

I cannot thank my agent, Kristyn Benton, and publisher, Rebecca Kaplan, enough for believing in my story and this book. To Kathryn O'Shea Evans, for your expertise and wonderful help in the creation of this project.

For my photographers—Katie Nixon, Rebekah Westover, Cassidy Brown, Cedric Klein, and Elijah Hoffman. Katie Nixon—for taking on the vast majority of this project, what fun it is has been to work with you for the last five years.

My parents, Roger and Kathryn Carter, for your endless love and for showing me that my dreams could be a reality. Your passions, curiosity, work ethic, and love for travel make me who I am, and your encouragement is everything. I see the world the way I do because of you.

To my siblings, the extended Carter family, and the Wilson family—I am so proud to be one of you!

My loyal friends and clients near and far, thank you for following along and lifting me up with encouragement and support for more than a decade. My faithful friends, you know who you are, your unwavering friendships mean everything to me—thank you for being a sounding board and showing up in my life (and at my grand openings!).

My CW team, you make magic happen each and every day for our customers and stores—and that makes the Caitlin Wilson brand a true success. Nicole Ray, whose artistry and talent brings my ideas to life—her dedication to the team and friendship is unparalleled. To McCall Corbett, who helped tirelessly throughout the process on photos and graphics.

To my five children, Olivia, Penn, Chloe, Lucy, and Charlotte—you are my everything! I am your mother first, and raising you is my greatest privilege. I treasure the memories of creating and dreaming with you at my feet, on my lap, or on my hip. I thank God for giving me the ultimate experience of growing a family and pursuing my dreams at once. I honor my calling as your mother and hope that you'll see that your futures are as big as your imagination!

My husband, Brigham—our travels and adventures are what started this beautiful story. Your strength and constant love have given me the courage to keep creating. You have built this with me and stepped in at every point of growth and need. My dreams have wings because of you.

Special thanks to the following designers, homeowners, and locations for welcoming us into their spaces:

Pages 4, 241: Location: Kips Bay Decorator Show House; interior design: Bobbitt & Company
Pages 20, 231, 236, 246: Photography: Cedric Klein; Location: Ritz Paris
Pages 23, 45: Kelley Lynn Design
Pages 33–35, 198: Rebekah Westover
Pages 48, 52, 56–57, 124, 132–133, 217, 238: Allie Beth Allman on behalf of the Fisher family
Pages 60, 112, 126, 134–135, 138–139, 185, 193, 212–214: Jada Leigh Mowles
Page 96, far left: Elijah Hoffman
Pages 108, left; 110–111, 227: Alexandra Kaehler Design,

photography: Aimee Mazzenga; stylist: Cate Ragan
Pages 25, 36–37, 50, 129, 142, 167, 169, 237, 182–183: Courtney Petit Design
Pages 174, 183: Nick Brock Antiques
Pages 154, 155, 191, 203, 247, 254: Morgan Hunt Design
Page 29: Kips Bay Decorator Show House; interior design by Michael Aiduss Studio Interiors + Architecture
Pages 21, 150–151: Sloan Home
Page 241: Landscape design: From the Ground Up Landscape
Pages 220, 225, 226, 229, 233, 236; 239, bottom right: Photography: Cassidy Brown
Page 233: The Lanesborough London
Page 220: Peggy Porschen Belgravia
Pages 226, 229, 236: Ritz Paris
Pages 229, 239: Museé Nissim de Camondo

Thank you to Lori Lilley, Sarah Hopkins, and Kate Jaynes for the gorgeous florals! Thank you to Fenwick Fields for tabletop linens and styling on pages 138, 139, 140, 142.

Special thanks to:
Courtney Petit
Jada Leigh Mowles
Morgan Hunt
Kelley Lynn Ledford
Alexandra Kaehler
Vanessa Sloan

So much gratitude for my team:
McCall, Christopher, Jessica, Caleb, Ellie, Natalie, Charlotte, Charity, and styling by Nicole Ray. Big thanks to the families and darling children who were photographed.

Following page: A sentimental touch of her grandmother's wedding portrait hung by the bedside in Morgan Hunt's Dallas home.

Editor: Rebecca Kaplan
Design Manager: Jenice Kim
Managing Editor: Glenn Ramirez
Production Manager: Sarah Masterson Hally

Book design by Emily Wardwell

Library of Congress Control Number: 2022946065

ISBN: 978-1-4197-6587-2
eISBN: 979-8-88707-062-9

Text copyright © 2023 Caitlin Wilson

Cover © 2023 Abrams

Printed and bound in the United States
10 9 8 7 6 5 4 3 2 1

Abrams books are available at special discounts when purchased in quantity for premiums and promotions as well as fundraising or educational use. Special editions can also be created to specification. For details, contact specialsales@abramsbooks.com or the address below.

Abrams® is a registered trademark of Harry N. Abrams, Inc.

ABRAMS The Art of Books
195 Broadway, New York, NY 10007
abramsbooks.com